PARARESCUE JUMPERS

OUT OF A HURRICANE!

BY SARAH EASON
ILLUSTRATED BY DIEGO VIASBERG

BEARPORT
PUBLISHING

Minneapolis, Minnesota

Editor: Jennifer Sanderson
Proofreader: Harriet McGregor
Designer: Paul Myerscough

Credits: 20, © Senior Airman Jordan Castelan/U.S. Air Force; 21, © Master Sgt. Lance S. Cheung/U.S. Air Force; 22l, © Airman 1st Class Veronica Pierce/U.S. Air Force; 22tr, © Chrissy Cuttita/U.S. Air Force; 22c, © SSGT Andrew Hughan/U.S. Air Force; 22b, © Senior Airman Kenny Kennemer/U.S. Air Force.

DISCLAIMER: This graphic story is a dramatization based on true events. It is intended to give the reader a sense of the narrative rather than a presentation of actual details as they occurred.

Library of Congress Cataloging-in-Publication Data

Names: Eason, Sarah, author. | Viasberg, Diego, 1981- illustrator.
Title: Pararescue jumpers : out of a hurricane! / by Sarah Eason ;
   illustrations by Diego Viasberg.
Description: Minneapolis, Minnesota : Bearport Publishing Company, [2021] |
   Series: Mission: Special Ops | Includes bibliographical references and
   index. | Summary: U.S. Air Force pararescue jumper Keith Berry and his
   team fly into New Orleans and save those trapped by Hurricane Katrina in
   this graphic adventure. Includes information on pararescue jumpers and
   their equipment.
Identifiers: LCCN 2020030876 (print) | LCCN 2020030877 (ebook) | ISBN
   9781647476434 (library binding) | ISBN 9781647476502 (paperback) | ISBN
   9781647476571 (ebook)
Subjects: LCSH: United States Air Force—Parachute troops—Juvenile
   fiction. | United States Air Force—Search and rescue
   operations—Juvenile fiction. | Hurricane Katrina, 2005—Juvenile
   fiction. | Graphic novels. | CYAC: Graphic novels. | United States Air
   Force—Parachute troops—Fiction. | United States Air Force—Search and
   rescue operations—Fiction. | Hurricane Katrina, 2005—Fiction. | Rescue
   work—Fiction.
Classification: LCC PZ7.7.E173 Pat 2021 (print) | LCC PZ7.7.E173 (ebook)
   | DDC 741.5/973—dc23
LC record available at https://lccn.loc.gov/2020030876
LC ebook record available at https://lccn.loc.gov/2020030877

Copyright © 2021 Bearport Publishing Company. All rights reserved. No part of this publication may be reproduced in whole or in part, stored in any retrieval system, or transmitted in any form or by any means, electronic, mechanical, photocopying, recording, or otherwise, without written permission from the publisher.

For more information, write to Bearport Publishing, 5357 Penn Avenue South, Minneapolis, MN 55419.
Printed in the United States of America.

CONTENTS

Chapter One
Hurricane Horror 4

Chapter Two
The Hunt for Survivors 8

Chapter Three
Making It to Safety 12

Chapter Four
Many Lives Saved 16

Pararescue Jumpers 20
PJ Gear 22
Glossary 23
Index 24
Read More 24
Learn More Online 24

CHAPTER ONE

HURRICANE HORROR

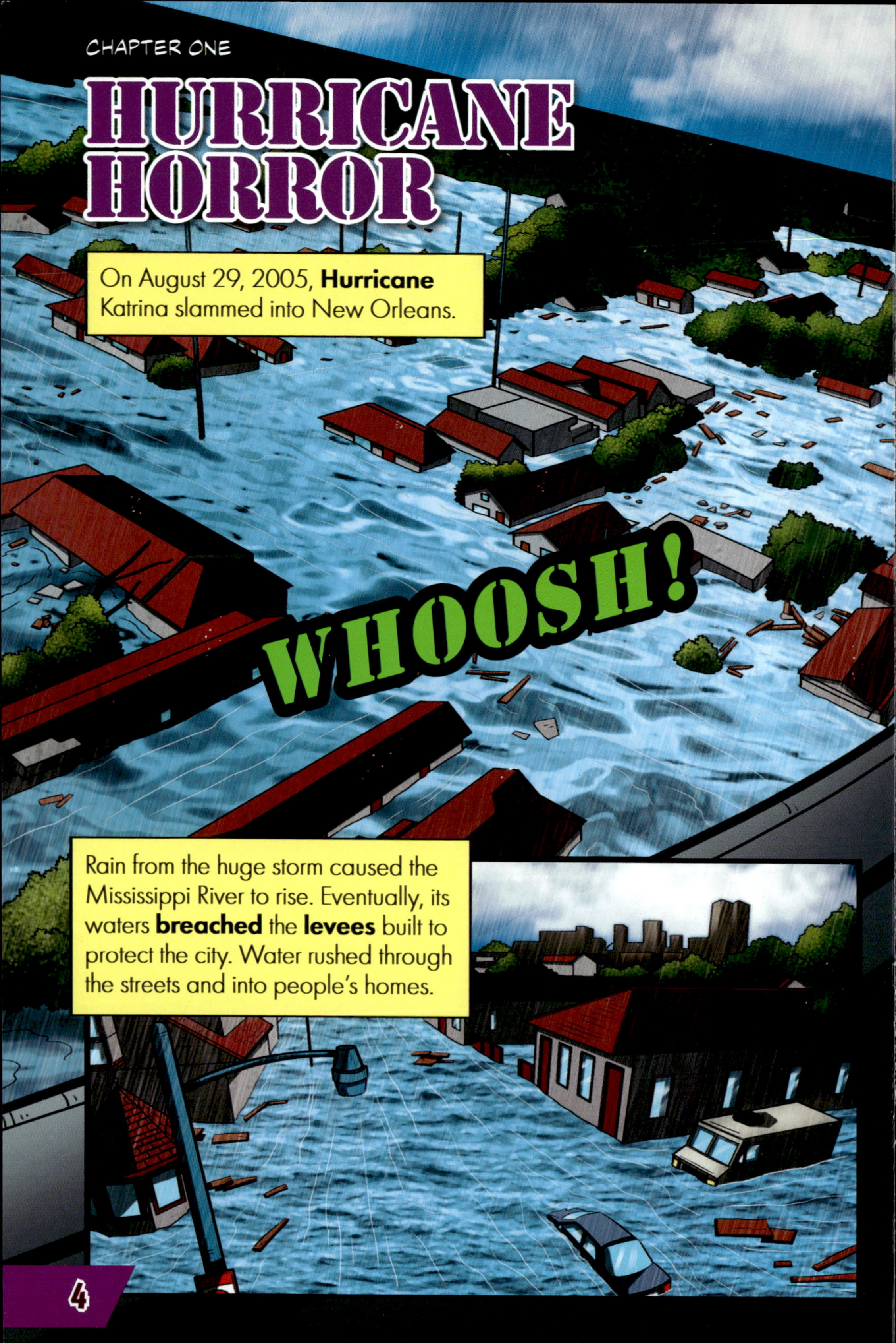
On August 29, 2005, **Hurricane** Katrina slammed into New Orleans.
WHOOSH!
Rain from the huge storm caused the Mississippi River to rise. Eventually, its waters **breached** the **levees** built to protect the city. Water rushed through the streets and into people's homes.

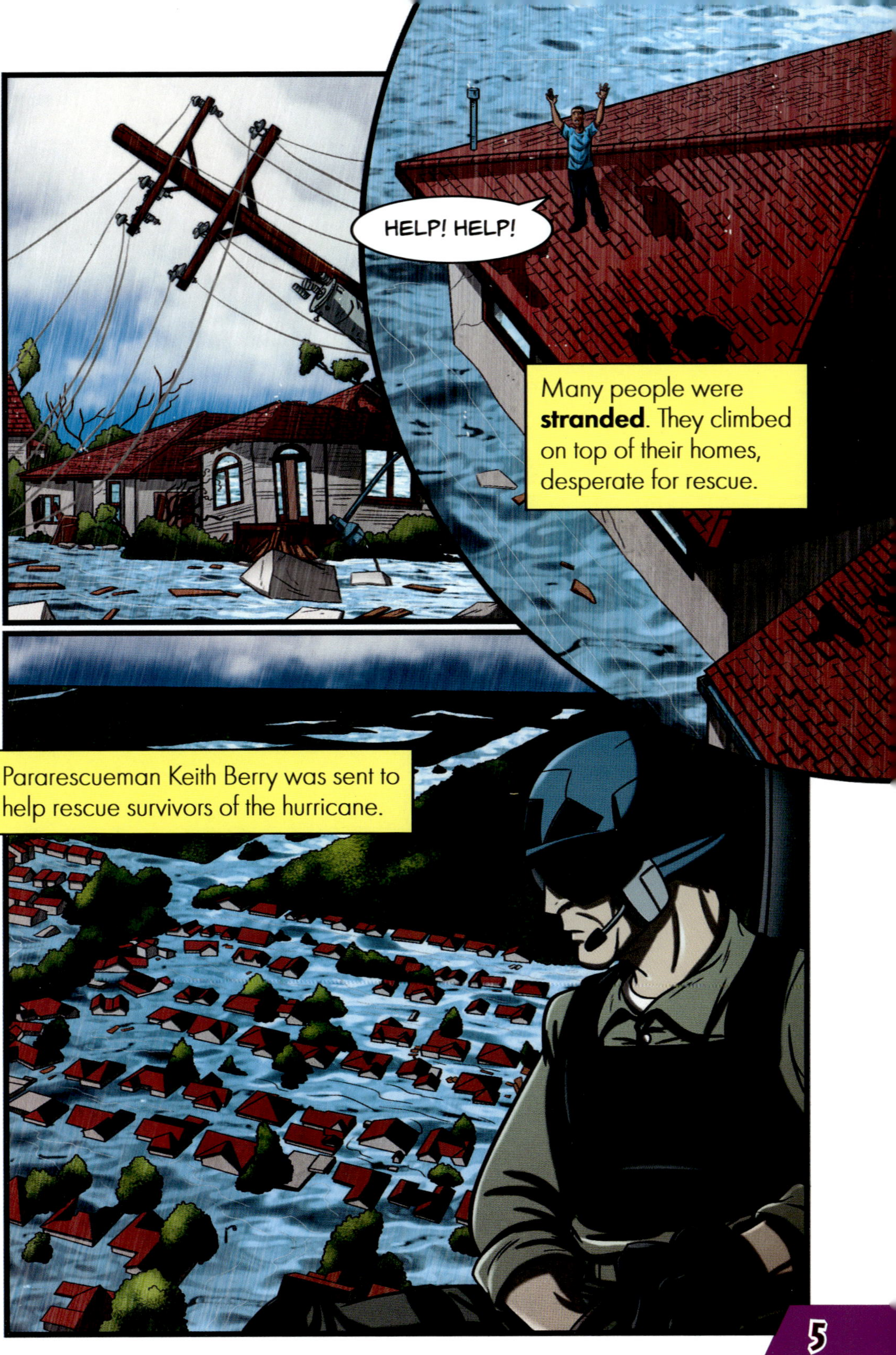
HELP! HELP!
Many people were **stranded**. They climbed on top of their homes, desperate for rescue.
Pararescueman Keith Berry was sent to help rescue survivors of the hurricane.

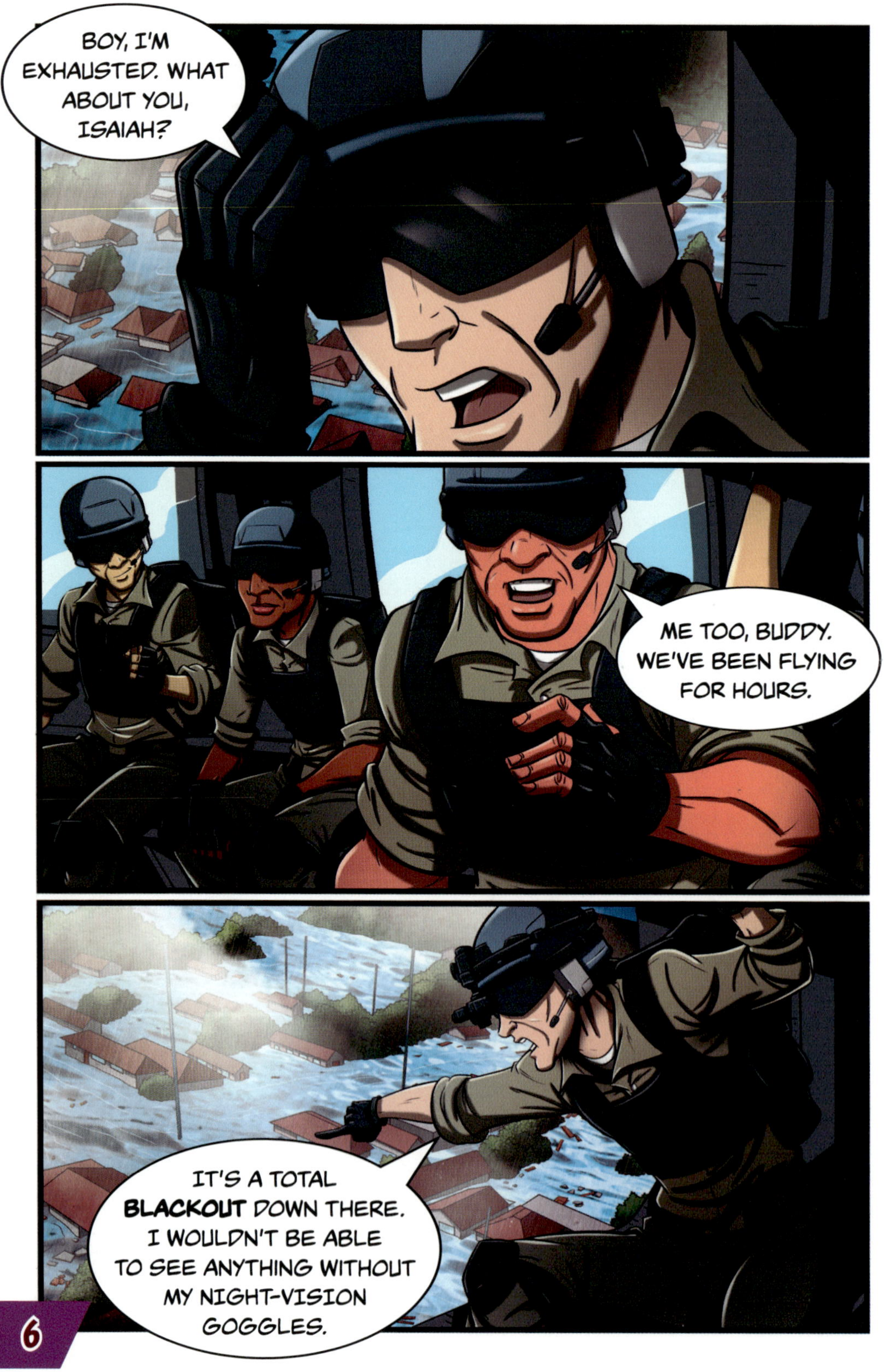
BOY, I'M EXHAUSTED. WHAT ABOUT YOU, ISAIAH?
ME TOO, BUDDY. WE'VE BEEN FLYING FOR HOURS.
IT'S A TOTAL **BLACKOUT** DOWN THERE. I WOULDN'T BE ABLE TO SEE ANYTHING WITHOUT MY NIGHT-VISION GOGGLES.

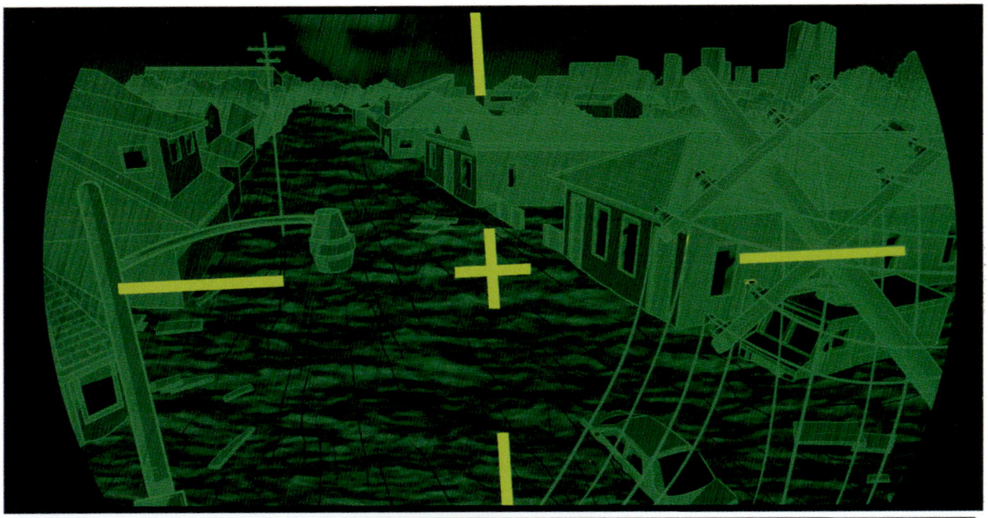

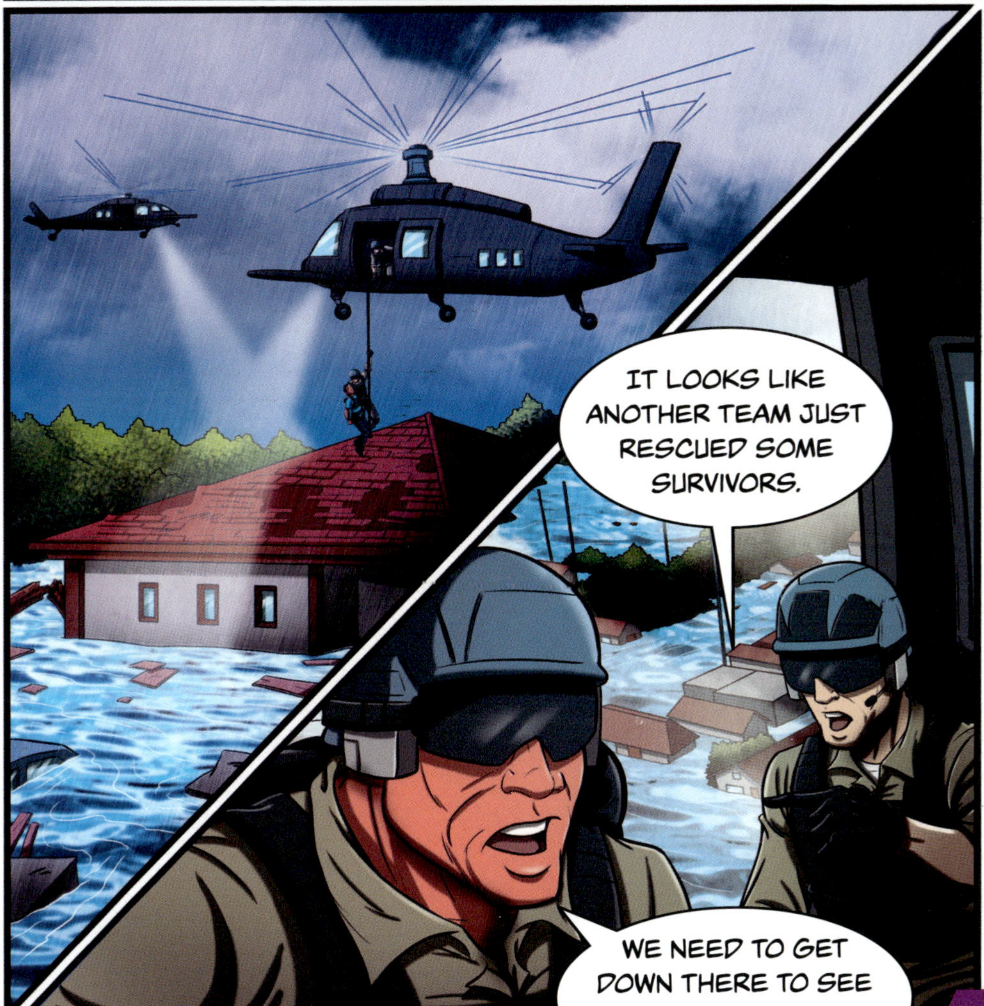
IT LOOKS LIKE ANOTHER TEAM JUST RESCUED SOME SURVIVORS.
WE NEED TO GET DOWN THERE TO SEE IF THERE ARE MORE IN THE AREA!

CHAPTER TWO

THE HUNT FOR SURVIVORS

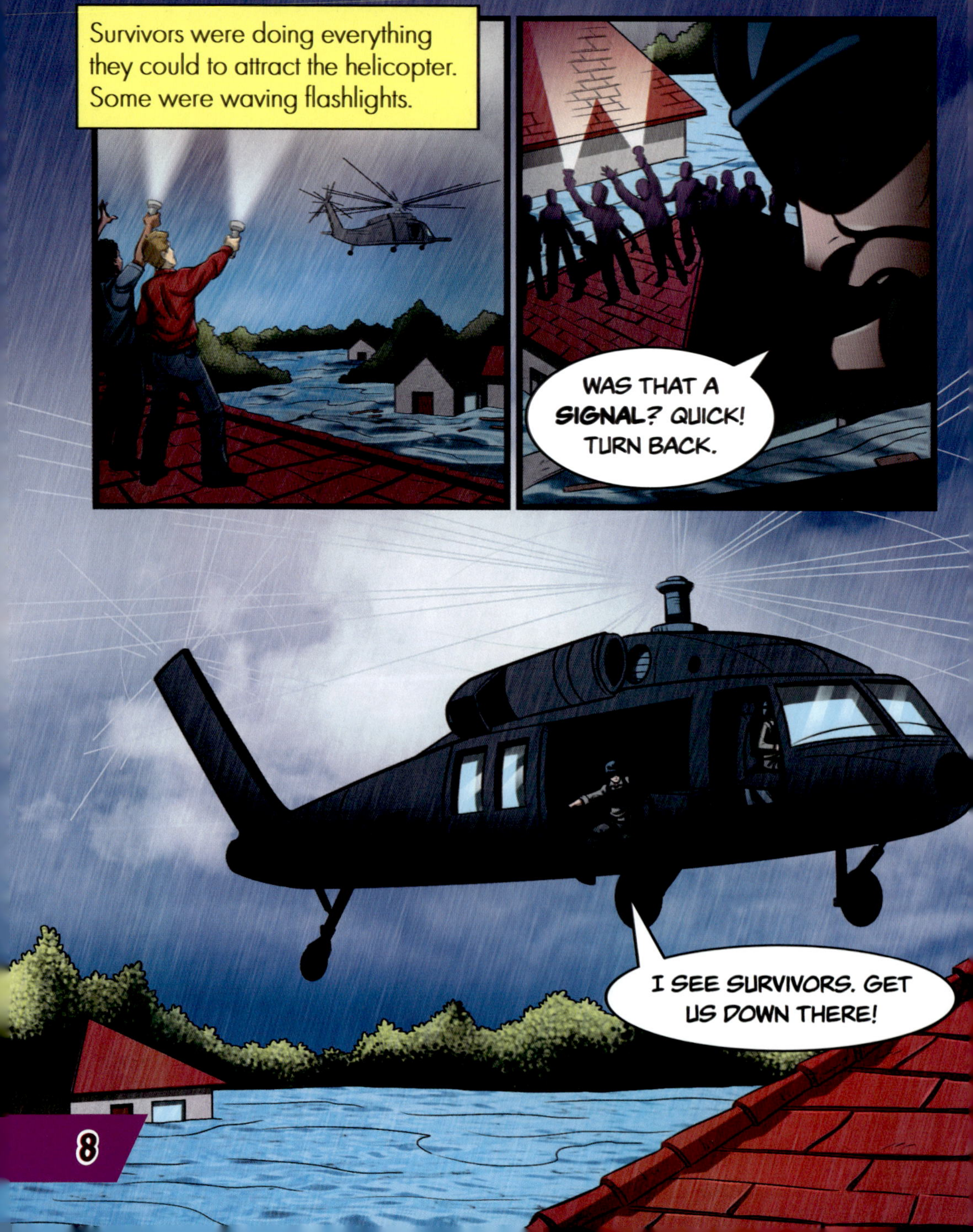

Survivors were doing everything they could to attract the helicopter. Some were waving flashlights.
WAS THAT A SIGNAL? QUICK! TURN BACK.
I SEE SURVIVORS. GET US DOWN THERE!

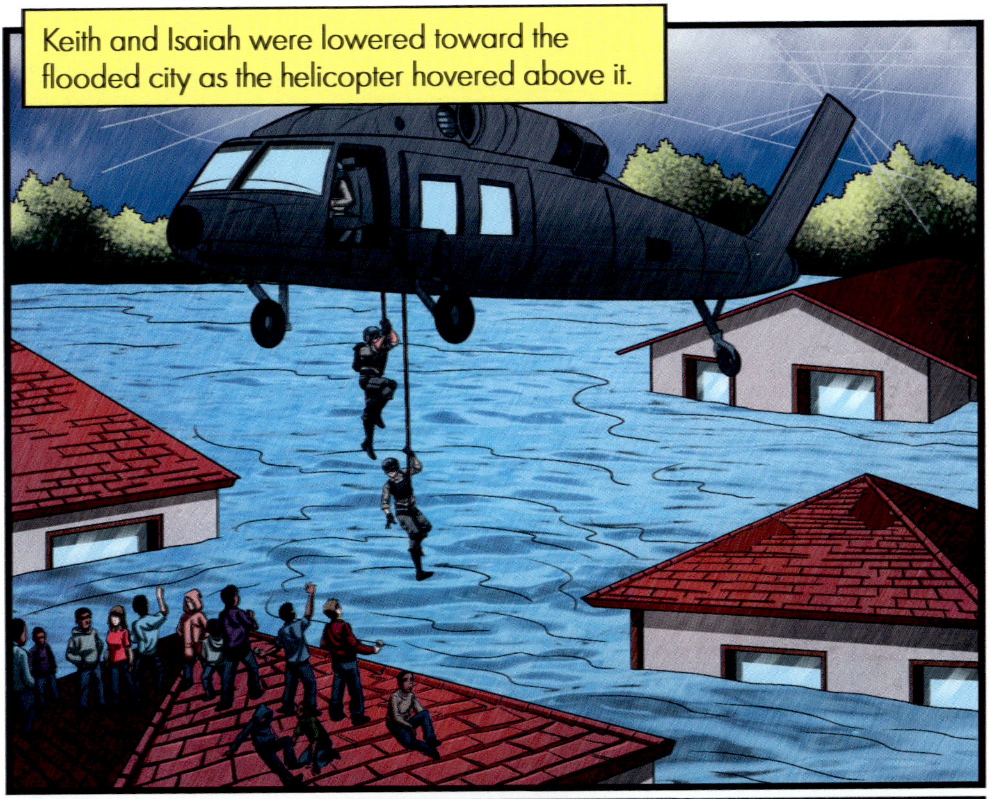
Keith and Isaiah were lowered toward the flooded city as the helicopter hovered above it.

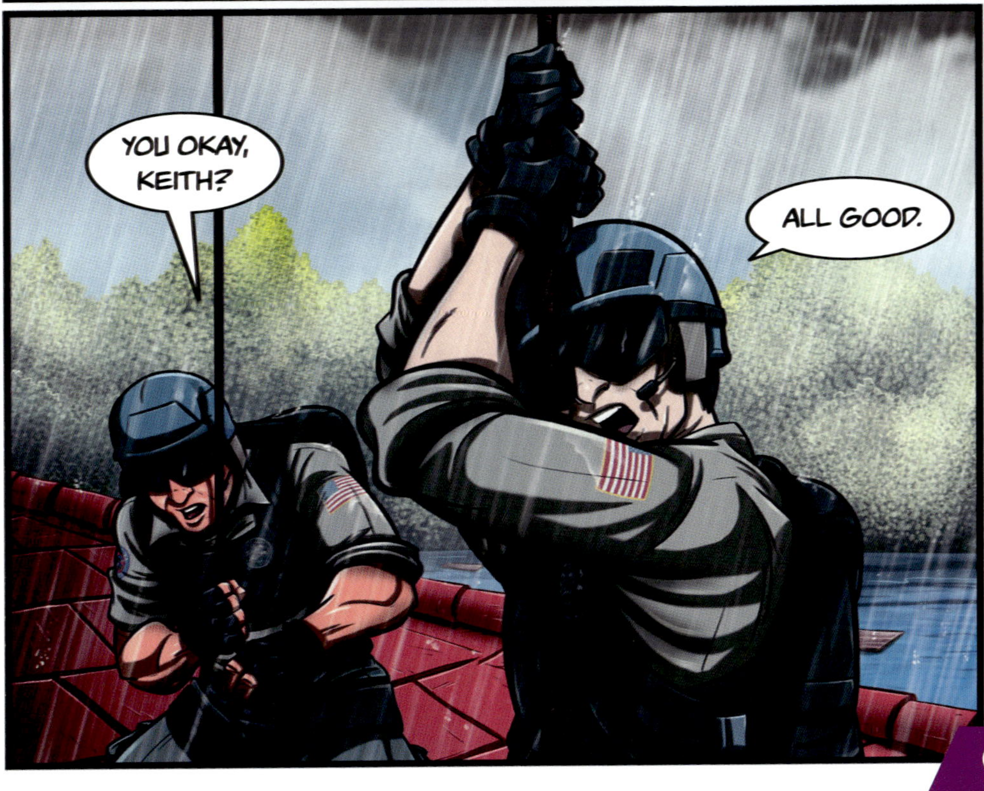
YOU OKAY, KEITH?
ALL GOOD.

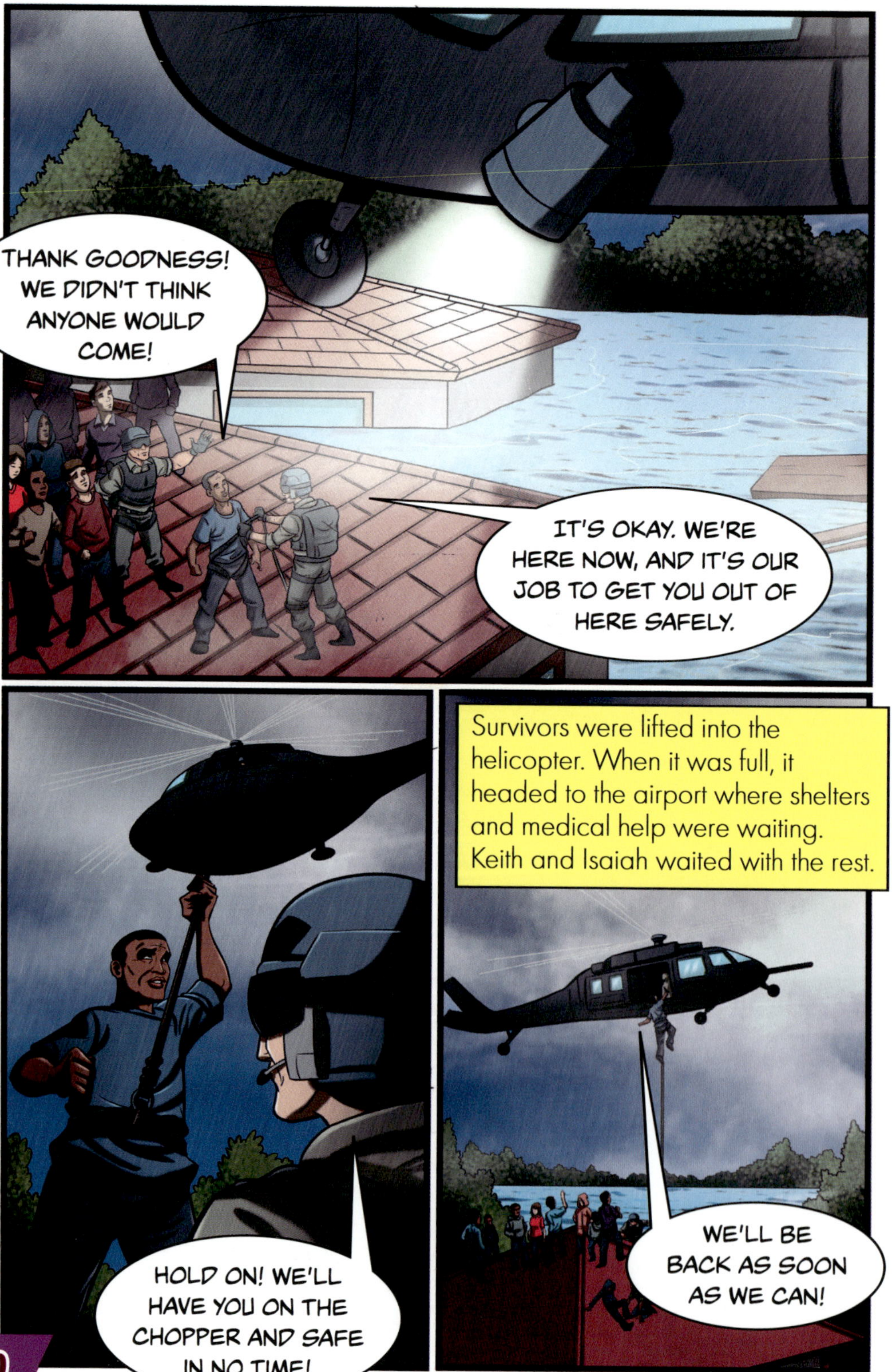
THANK GOODNESS! WE DIDN'T THINK ANYONE WOULD COME!
IT'S OKAY. WE'RE HERE NOW, AND IT'S OUR JOB TO GET YOU OUT OF HERE SAFELY.
HOLD ON! WE'LL HAVE YOU ON THE CHOPPER AND SAFE IN NO TIME!
Survivors were lifted into the helicopter. When it was full, it headed to the airport where shelters and medical help were waiting. Keith and Isaiah waited with the rest.
WE'LL BE BACK AS SOON AS WE CAN!

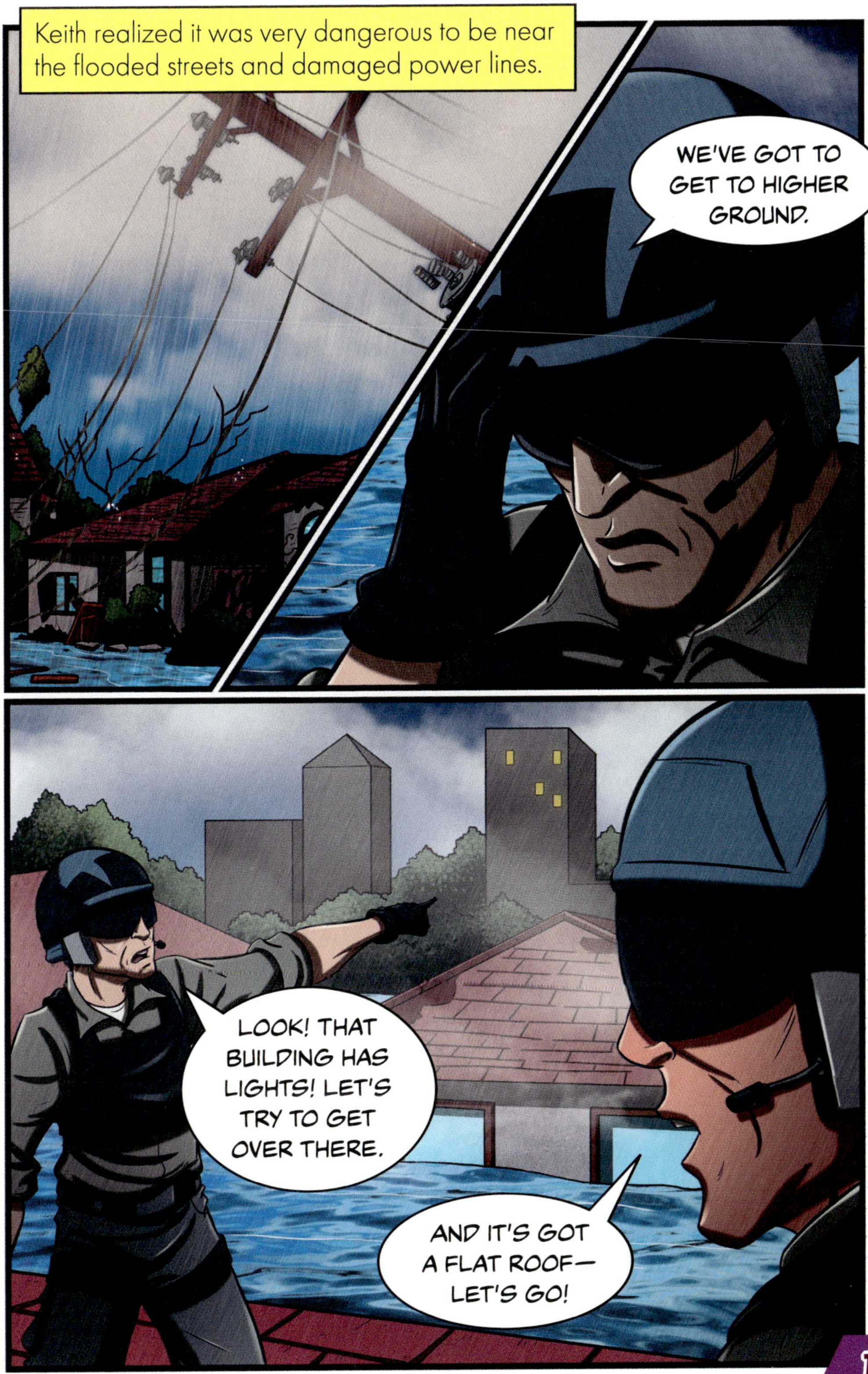
Keith realized it was very dangerous to be near the flooded streets and damaged power lines.
WE'VE GOT TO GET TO HIGHER GROUND.
LOOK! THAT BUILDING HAS LIGHTS! LET'S TRY TO GET OVER THERE.
AND IT'S GOT A FLAT ROOF—LET'S GO!

MAKING IT TO SAFETY

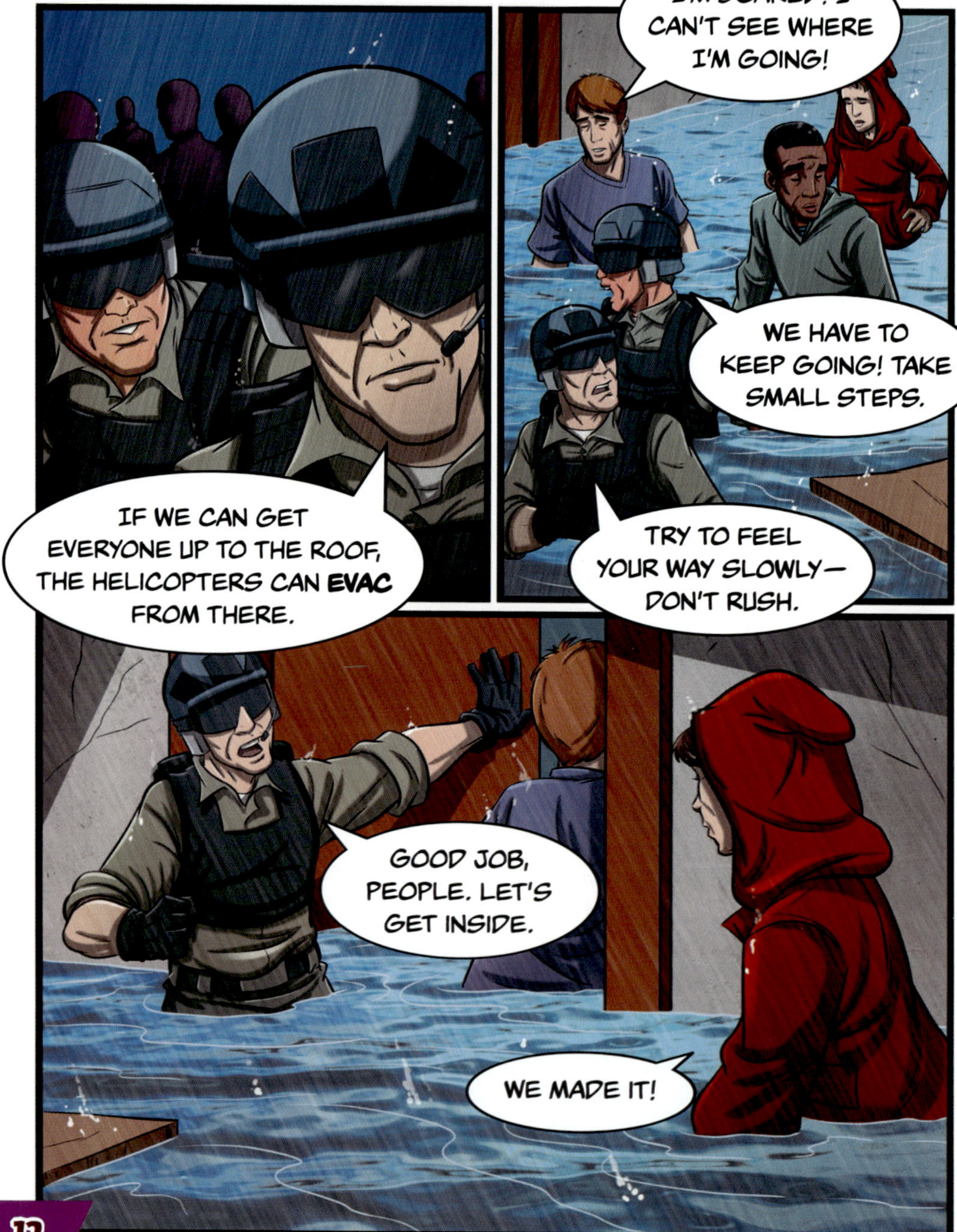
IF WE CAN GET EVERYONE UP TO THE ROOF, THE HELICOPTERS CAN **EVAC** FROM THERE.
I'M SCARED! I CAN'T SEE WHERE I'M GOING!
WE HAVE TO KEEP GOING! TAKE SMALL STEPS.
TRY TO FEEL YOUR WAY SLOWLY— DON'T RUSH.
GOOD JOB, PEOPLE. LET'S GET INSIDE.
WE MADE IT!

Inside the building, more survivors were waiting for help.

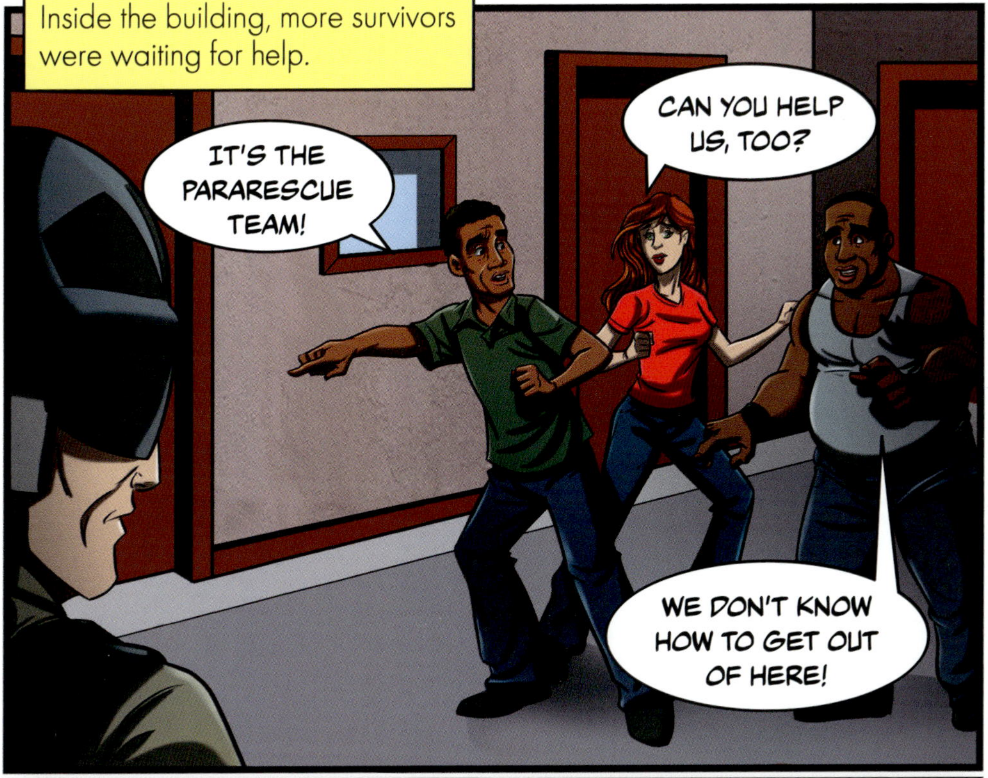
IT'S THE PARARESCUE TEAM!
CAN YOU HELP US, TOO?
WE DON'T KNOW HOW TO GET OUT OF HERE!

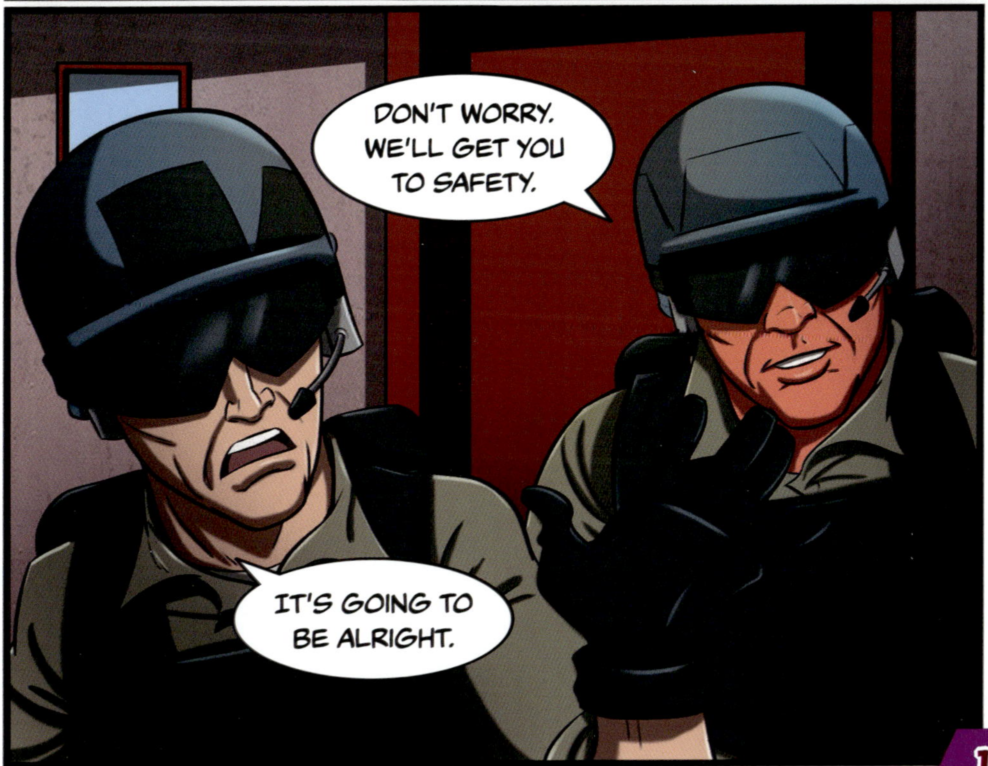
DON'T WORRY. WE'LL GET YOU TO SAFETY.
IT'S GOING TO BE ALRIGHT.

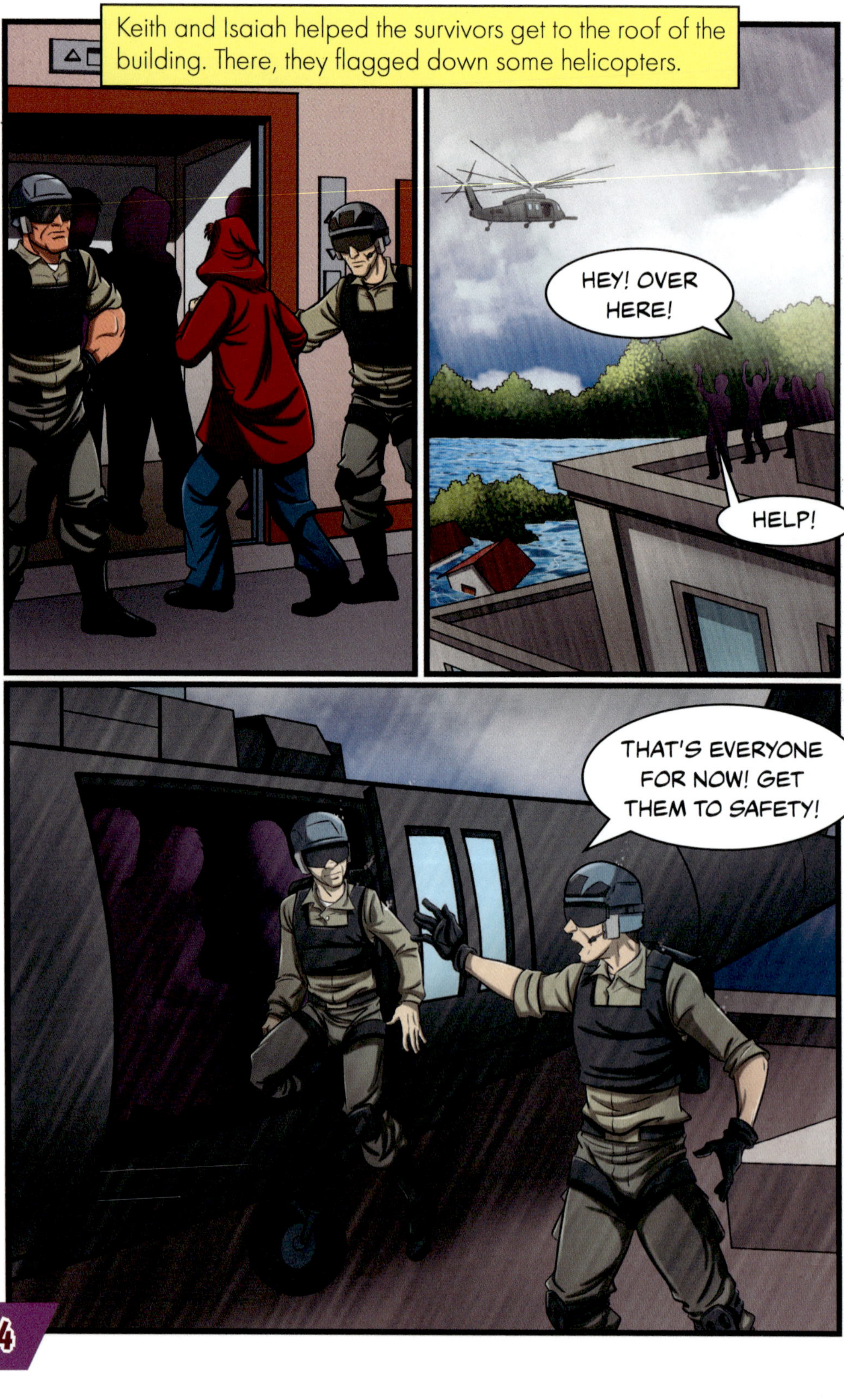
Keith and Isaiah helped the survivors get to the roof of the building. There, they flagged down some helicopters.
HEY! OVER HERE!
HELP!
THAT'S EVERYONE FOR NOW! GET THEM TO SAFETY!

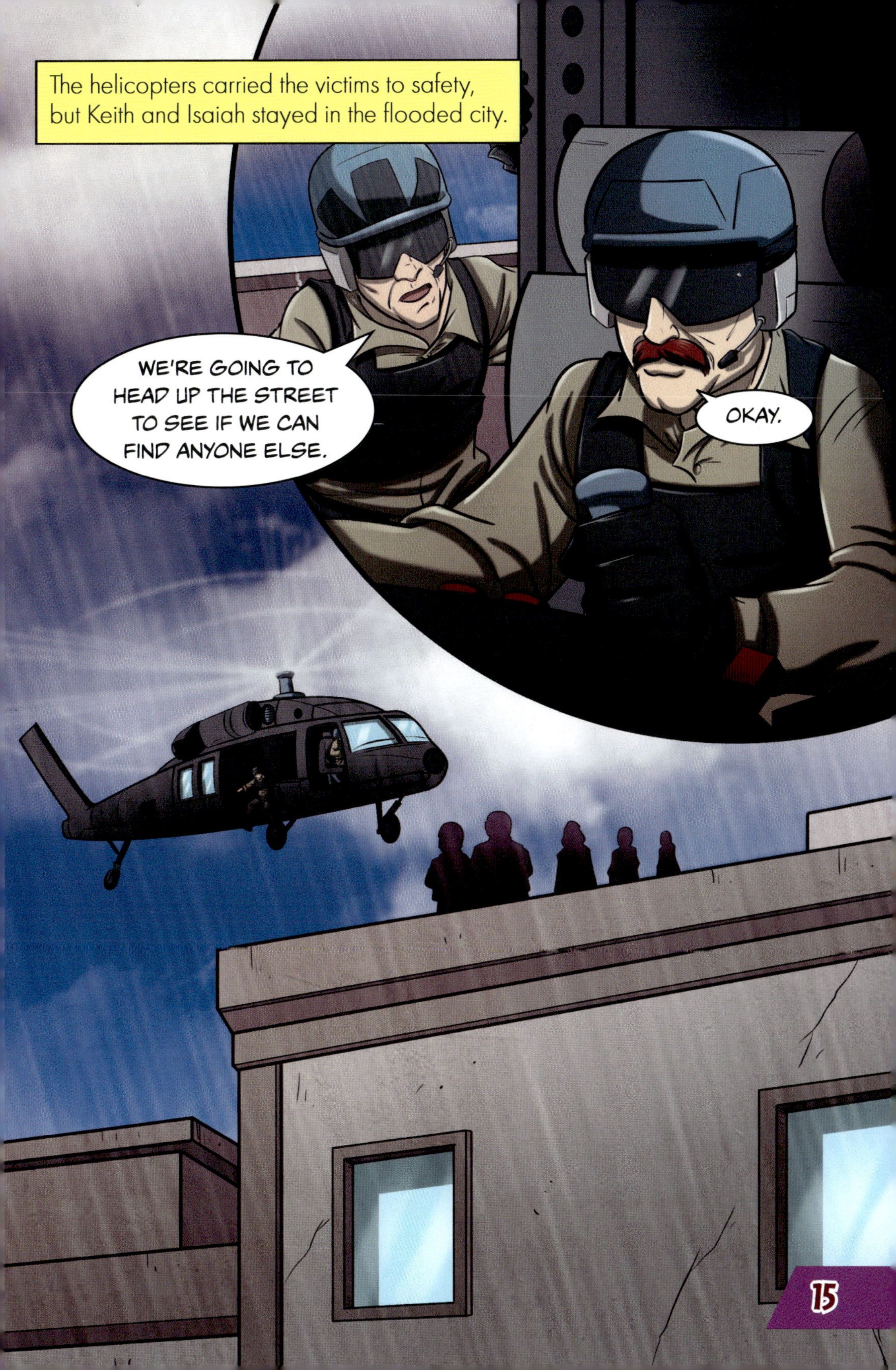
The helicopters carried the victims to safety, but Keith and Isaiah stayed in the flooded city.
WE'RE GOING TO HEAD UP THE STREET TO SEE IF WE CAN FIND ANYONE ELSE.
OKAY.

CHAPTER FOUR

MANY LIVES SAVED

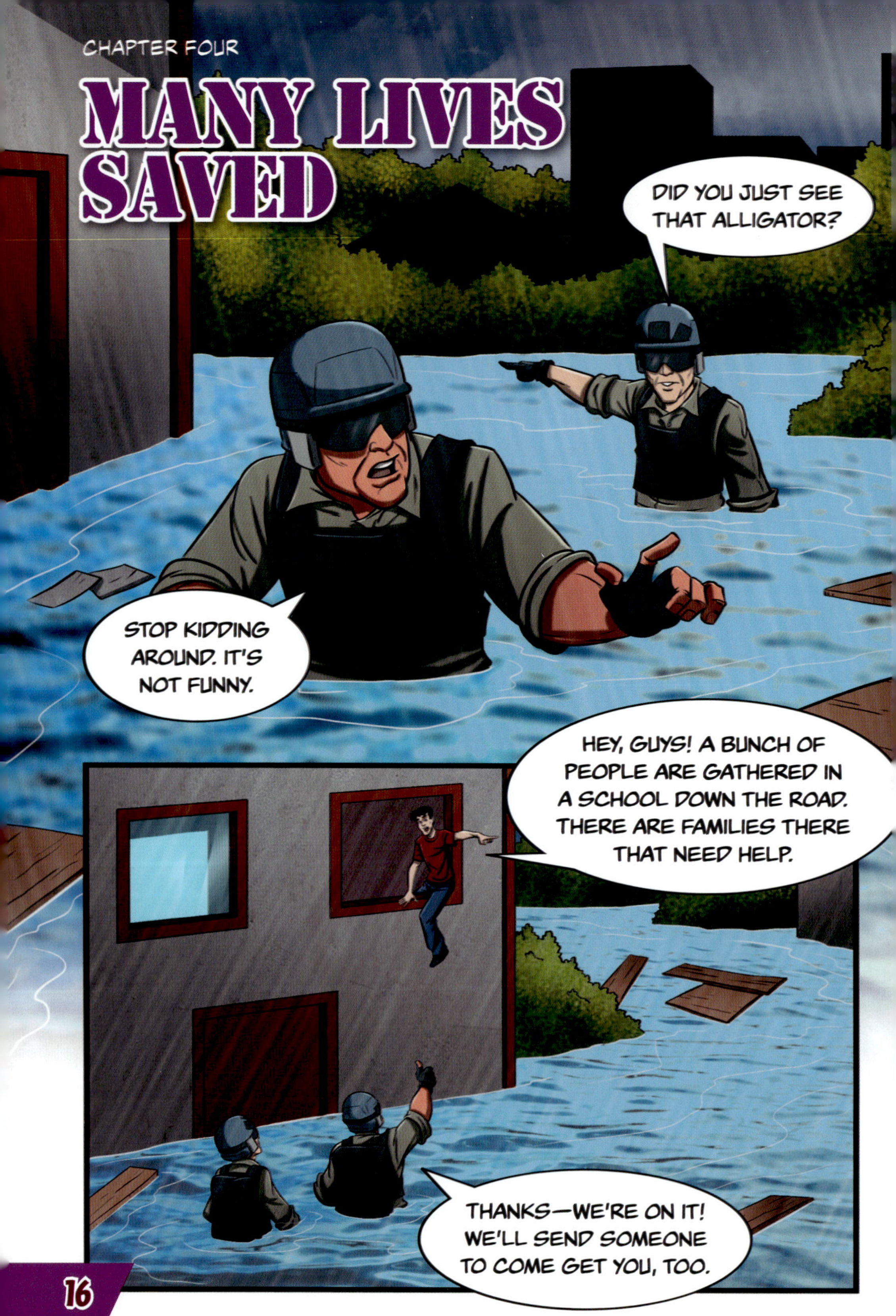
DID YOU JUST SEE THAT ALLIGATOR?
STOP KIDDING AROUND. IT'S NOT FUNNY.
HEY, GUYS! A BUNCH OF PEOPLE ARE GATHERED IN A SCHOOL DOWN THE ROAD. THERE ARE FAMILIES THERE THAT NEED HELP.
THANKS—WE'RE ON IT! WE'LL SEND SOMEONE TO COME GET YOU, TOO.

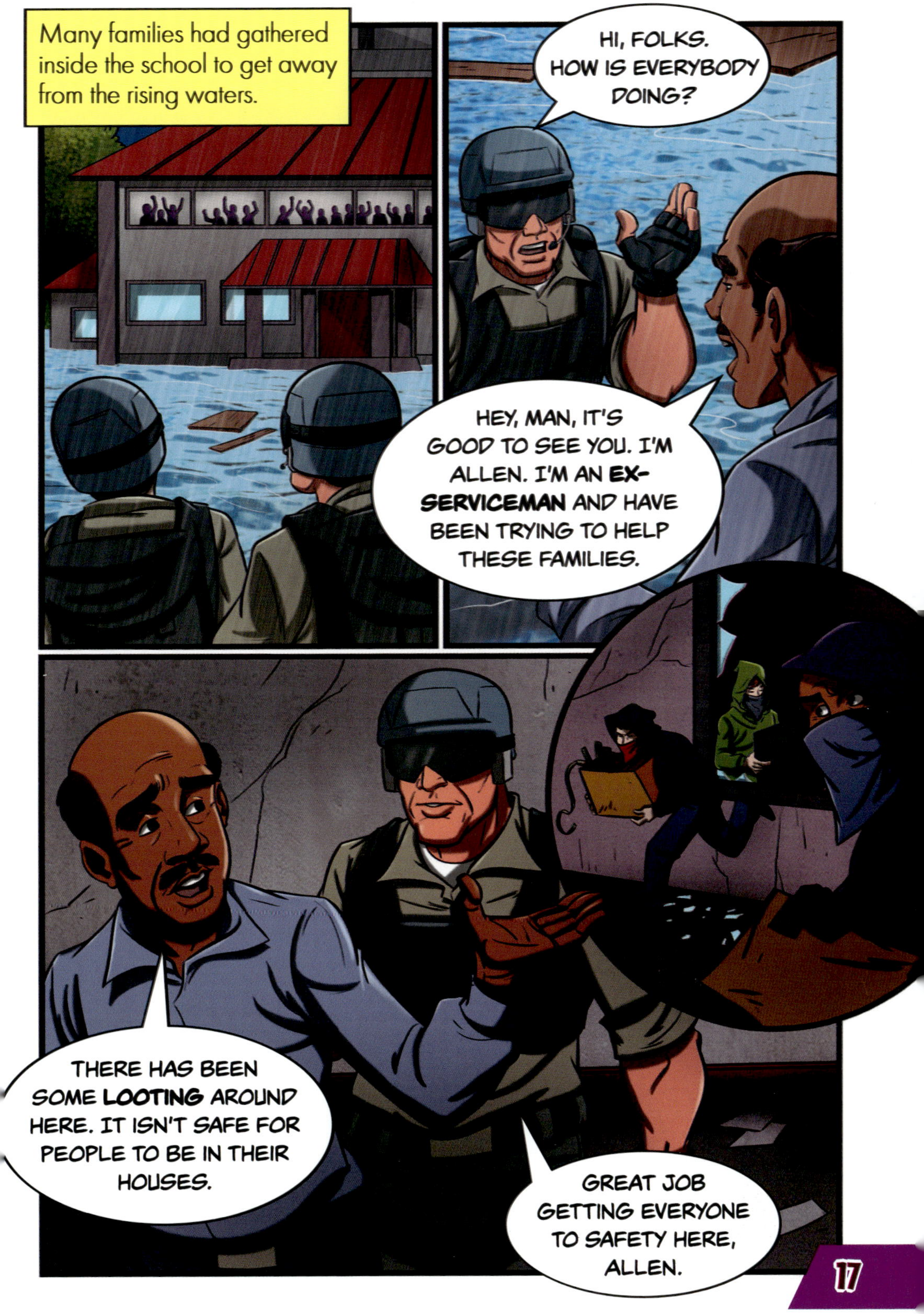
Many families had gathered inside the school to get away from the rising waters.
HI, FOLKS. HOW IS EVERYBODY DOING?
HEY, MAN, IT'S GOOD TO SEE YOU. I'M ALLEN. I'M AN EX-SERVICEMAN AND HAVE BEEN TRYING TO HELP THESE FAMILIES.
THERE HAS BEEN SOME LOOTING AROUND HERE. IT ISN'T SAFE FOR PEOPLE TO BE IN THEIR HOUSES.
GREAT JOB GETTING EVERYONE TO SAFETY HERE, ALLEN.

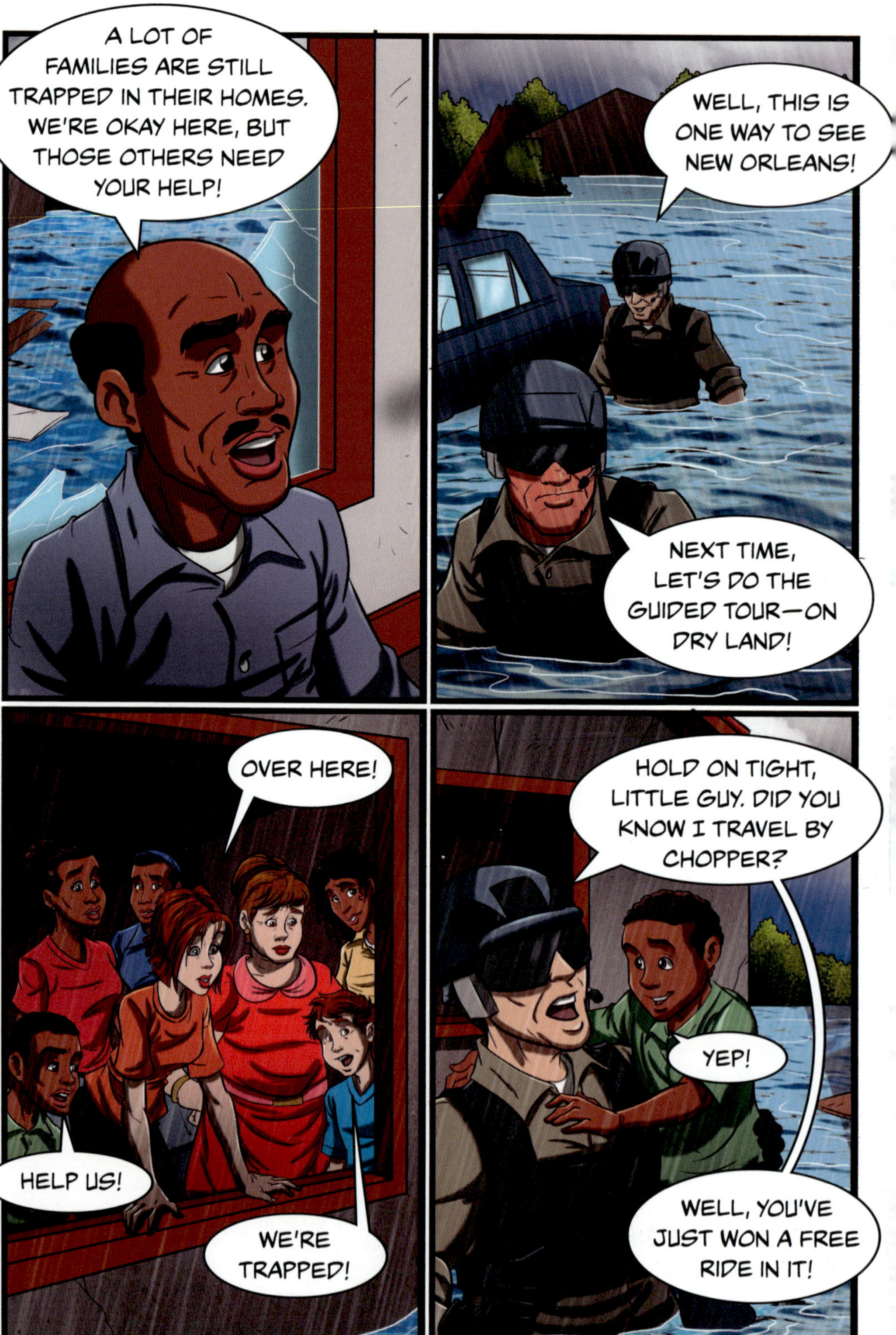
A LOT OF FAMILIES ARE STILL TRAPPED IN THEIR HOMES. WE'RE OKAY HERE, BUT THOSE OTHERS NEED YOUR HELP!
WELL, THIS IS ONE WAY TO SEE NEW ORLEANS!
NEXT TIME, LET'S DO THE GUIDED TOUR—ON DRY LAND!
OVER HERE!
HELP US!
WE'RE TRAPPED!
HOLD ON TIGHT, LITTLE GUY. DID YOU KNOW I TRAVEL BY CHOPPER?
YEP!
WELL, YOU'VE JUST WON A FREE RIDE IN IT!

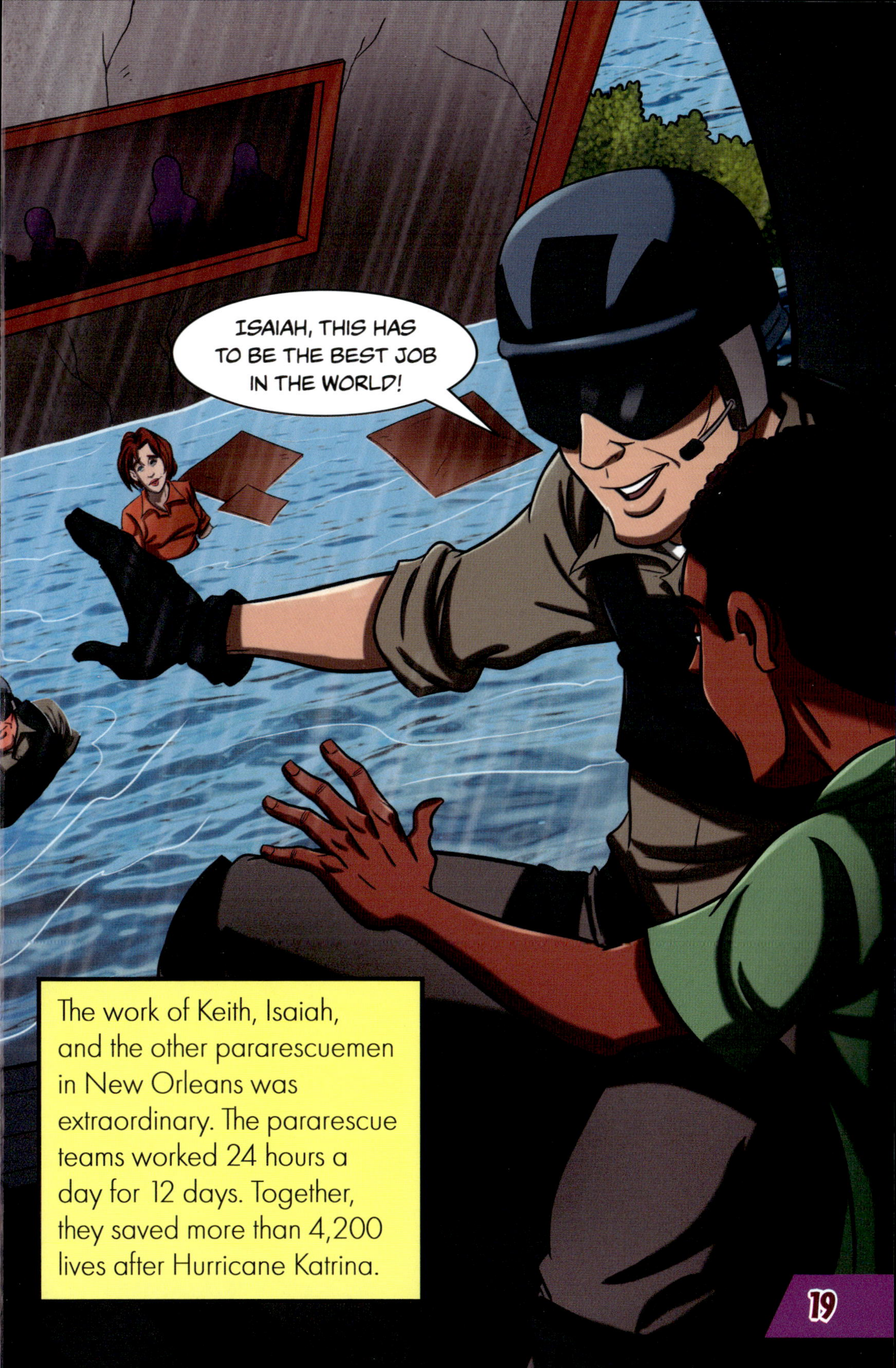
ISAIAH, THIS HAS TO BE THE BEST JOB IN THE WORLD!
The work of Keith, Isaiah, and the other pararescuemen in New Orleans was extraordinary. The pararescue teams worked 24 hours a day for 12 days. Together, they saved more than 4,200 lives after Hurricane Katrina.

PARARESCUE JUMPERS

Pararescue jumpers, or PJs, are part of a special operations team for the U.S. Air Force. They are called jumpers because they often jump from planes or helicopters and use parachutes to get to the ground. Trained in medical, survival, and combat skills, PJs perform some of the world's toughest rescues.

IT TAKES A LOT OF EXTRA TRAINING TO BECOME A PJ. THEY ARE THE BEST OF THE BEST.

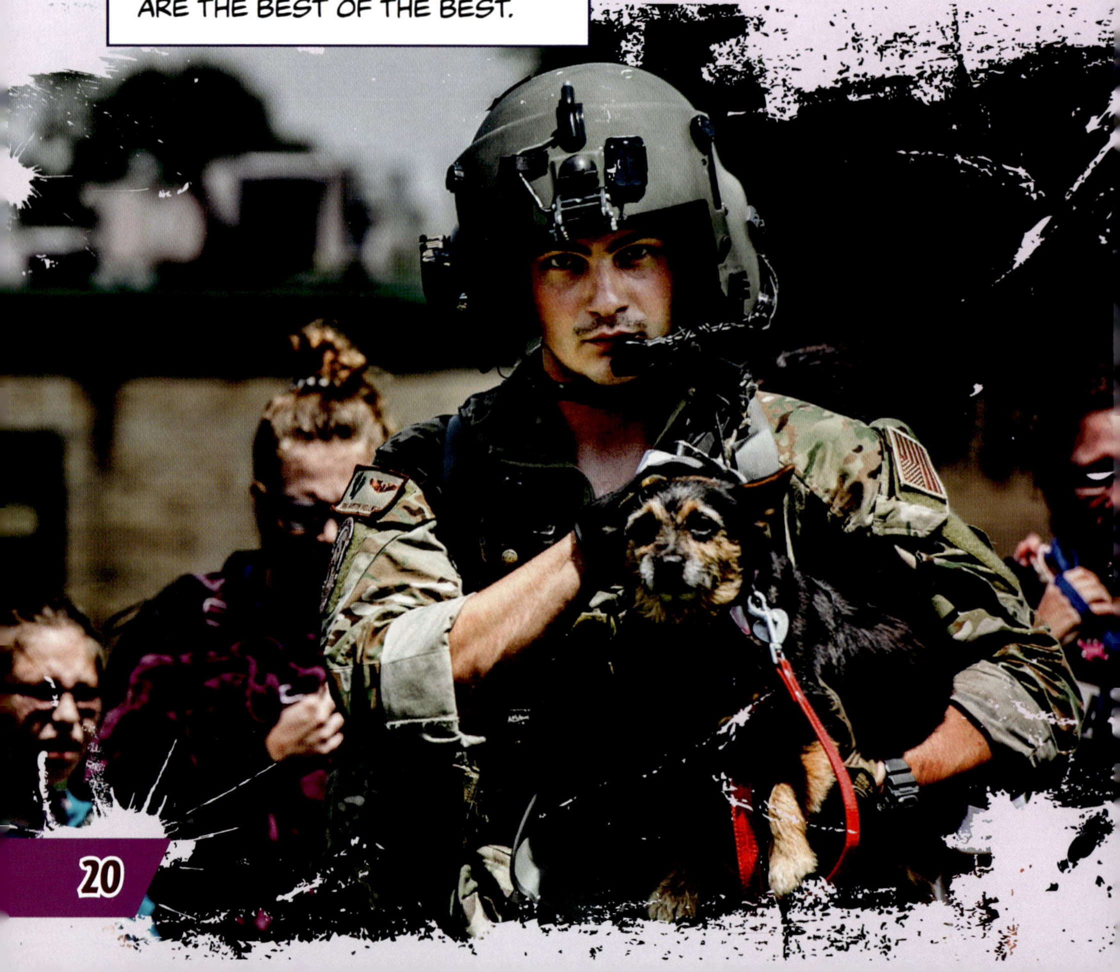

PJS CAN PARACHUTE UP TO 25,000 FEET (7,620 M) FROM AIRPLANES. THEY ALSO JUMP INTO RAGING SEAS AND BRAVE **BLIZZARDS** ON THE HIGHEST MOUNTAINTOPS.

Many pararescue missions happen in the middle of war. If a plane goes down, the PJs search for stranded airmen. They care for the wounded. They may even have to fight the enemy.

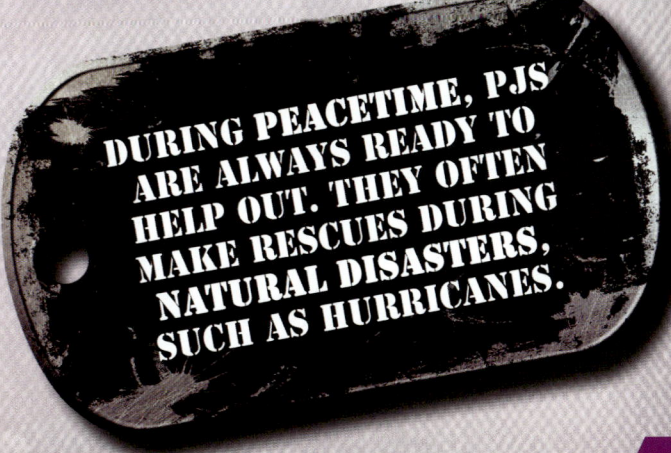

DURING PEACETIME, PJS ARE ALWAYS READY TO HELP OUT. THEY OFTEN MAKE RESCUES DURING NATURAL DISASTERS, SUCH AS HURRICANES.

PJ GEAR

PJs use a lot of equipment to carry out their missions. Here is some of the gear they use.

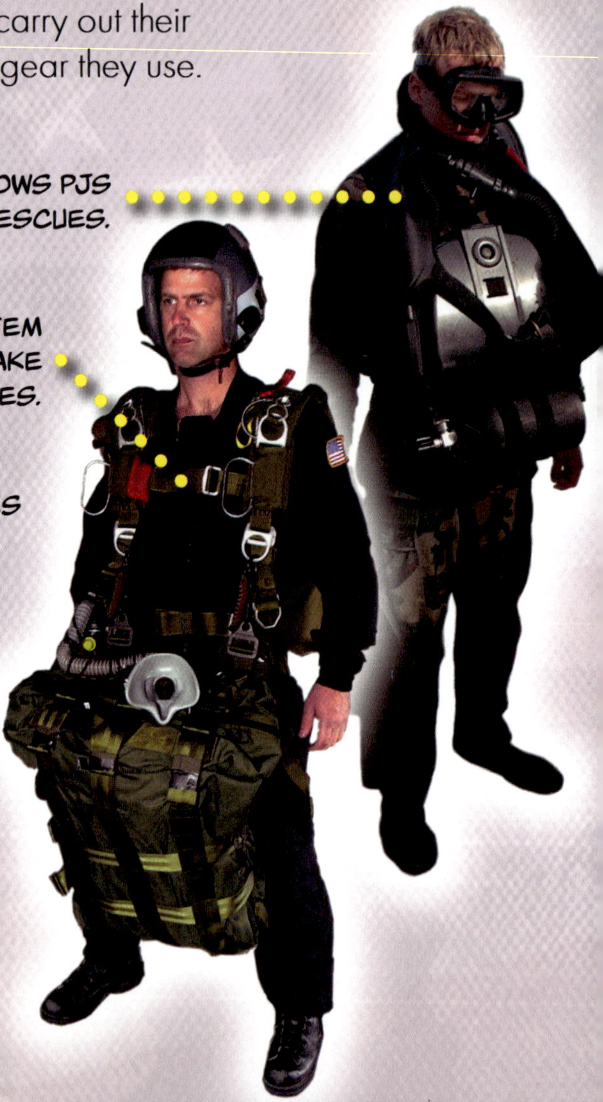

SCUBA EQUIPMENT ALLOWS PJS TO MAKE UNDERWATER RESCUES.

THE HALO PARACHUTE SYSTEM IS USED WHEN PJS NEED TO MAKE RESCUES BEHIND ENEMY LINES.

PJS CARRY MEDICAL BACKPACKS FILLED WITH ABOUT 80 POUNDS (36 KG) OF SUPPLIES.

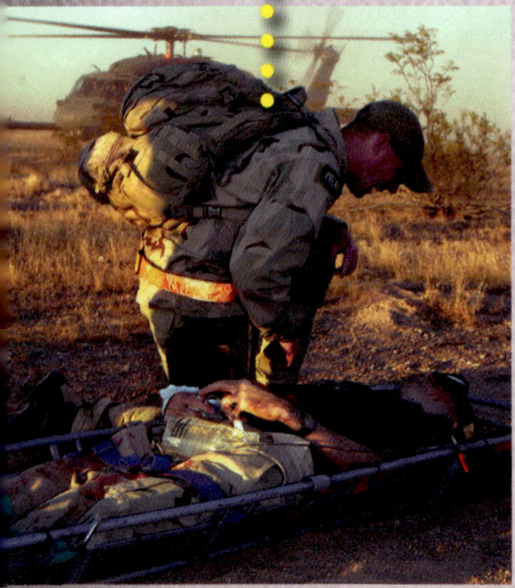

HH-60G PAVE HAWK HELICOPTERS TAKE PJS TO AND FROM RESCUE SITES.

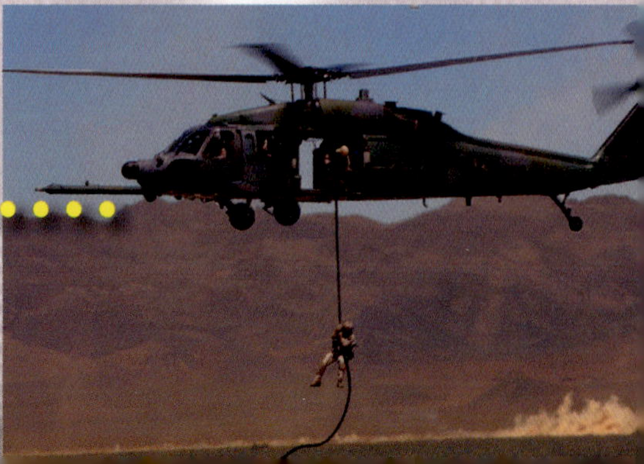

GLOSSARY

blackout a total loss of electricity, resulting in no lights

blizzards very heavy snowstorms with strong winds

breached pushed through and over

evac short for evacuate; to move away from a dangerous area

ex-serviceman a person who was once in the armed forces

hurricane a violent storm with very high winds and heavy rain

levees walls built near a city to try to protect it from the water of a river when it bursts its banks; there are levees to protect New Orleans from the water of the Mississippi River

looting stealing things during times of trouble, such as during a natural disaster

natural disasters events caused by weather or nature that result in great damage or loss

peacetime a time during which a country is not at war

signal a sign to tell someone something

stranded stuck somewhere without a way to leave

INDEX

blackout 6
evac 12
halo parachute 22
helicopter 8–10, 12, 14–15, 20, 22
Hurricane Katrina 4, 19
levees 4
looting 17
medical backpacks 22
Mississippi River 4
New Orleans 4, 18–19
night-vision goggles 6
scuba equipment 22
signal 8
survivors 5, 7–8, 10, 13–14

READ MORE

Gagliardi, Sue. *Hurricane Katrina (21st Century Disasters)*. Mendota Heights, MN: North Star Editions, 2019.

Garstecki, Julia. *U.S. Air Force (U.S. Military Forces)*. Mankato, MN: Black Rabbit Books, 2021.

Mattern, Joanne. *The Science of Hurricanes (The Science of Natural Disasters)*. New York: Cavendish Square Publishing, 2019.

LEARN MORE ONLINE

1. Go to www.factsurfer.com
2. Enter **"Out of Hurricane"** into the search box.
3. Click on the cover of this book to see a list of websites.